CW00486274

100 FACTS, MYTHS & LEGENDS ABOUT THE COTSWOLDS

Matt Cass & Paul James

This book is dedicated to the wonderful Cotswolds and to all the interesting characters, facts, myths and stories that make it such a special place; without them we could not have written this book.

Thanks also to our wives and families who have helped, questioned and challenged us and made their own suggestions (polite and otherwise!) while we have been compiling this book.

INTRODUCTION

The first of our '**100 Facts, Myths and Legends**' books was about our home city of Gloucester. It seemed logical that the second in the series should be about **The Cotswolds** - an area not far away, which has an equally rich seam of potential content.

Co-author **Paul James** has worked heading up economic development for **Cotswold District Council** since 2020 so has picked up some of what is in this book during his time in that role. The rest of it has required more research, which has been an education as well as fascinating and fun.

Fellow author **Matt Cass**, a director of a family-owned independent insurance brokers business in Gloucester, has walked the 102 mile **Cotswold Way** in 7 days. He revisited parts of it when completing the route of 100 mile **Gloucestershire Way** to raise funds for the Gloucester-based charity The Spring Centre in 2011.

We'd like to thank everyone who has helped us put this together, including **Cotswolds Tourism** and the three photographers, **Anthony Paul, Nick Turner and Emma Bidmead**, for supplying photographic images. They are very talented, so do please check out their websites -

www.anthonypaulphotography.com

www.nickturnerphoto.com

www.byemmajane.co.uk

Cotswolds Tourism's website is also a wealth of information about the area.

www.cotswolds.com

We hope you enjoy reading this book, that you learn things that you didn't know previously and that it prompts you to visit somewhere in the area that you haven't been before.

SYNOPSIS

The Cotswolds is one of the **UK's best-known and most-visited tourist destinations**, with an internationally-recognised brand. It is famous for rolling hills, beautiful countryside and stunning 'chocolate box' towns and villages. In fact, the name Cotswold is believed to mean '**sheep enclosure in rolling hillsides**' incorporating the term 'wold', **meaning hilly or rolling region**.

The Cotswolds is one of the country's largest **Areas of Outstanding Natural Beauty (AONB)**, covering almost 800 square miles and extending into five counties (Gloucestershire, Oxfordshire, Warwickshire, Wiltshire and Worcestershire). The 102-mile National Trail, the **Cotswold Way,** runs along the escarpment from the Roman city of Bath to the market town of Chipping Campden. There are plenty of sheep along the route - a reminder that the area originally derived its wealth from the wool trade.

But there's a lot more to it than that.   The

Cotswolds is a popular place to live, attracting the rich and famous. It is home to many historic buildings and monuments and has more than its fair share of quirky traditions and local legends. These days it even **has its own version of the board game Monopoly**, featuring many of the landmarks and attractions of the area.

The Cotswolds is also home to many innovative and successful businesses - more than most people realise.

This book celebrates the great things, as well as the quirky and lesser-known stories, about The Cotswolds.

CONTENTS

1 - BUILDINGS AND MONUMENTS

Tolkien's Door

The north porch of **St. Edward's Church** in **Stow-on-the-Wold** is home to a wooden door which, rumour has it, was the inspiration behind **J. R. R. Tolkien's Doors of Durin**, (also known as the West-gate, the West-door of Moria, or Elven Door), that appear in a scene in **'The Lord of the Rings: The Fellowship of the Ring'**.

Tolkien was known to visit the area while he studied at, and later became a professor at, **Oxford University**, but the claims have never been authenticated.

The north porch of the church was **built about 300 years ago** and young yew saplings were planted to enhance its entrance. Today these trees are now part of the architraves for the door and make this probably the most photographed door in the Cotswolds!

The door at St Edward's Church in Stow-on-the-Wold, which is said to have inspired J.R.R. Tolkien.

Credit: Cotswolds Tourism/ © Anthony Paul Photography

As Tall As Yew Like

Cirencester Park, the seat of the **Earl and Countess Bathurst**, is also home to the world's largest yew hedge. The **15,000 acre estate** has been in the Bathurst family for **over 325 years** having been bought by **Sir Benjamin Bathurst** in 1695.

The hedge can reach 40 feet tall before pruning. The cuttings gathered each year are sold to pharmaceutical companies as a **key ingredient used in cancer drugs**. The **compound paclitaxel (Taxol)** which is extracted from yew trees is used for **chemotherapy drugs** to fight several types of cancer.

The Yew hedge at Cirencester Park.

Credit: Cotswolds Tourism/ © Anthony Paul Photography

Does the King Live Above the Shop?

Highgrove, near **Tetbury**, has been home to **King Charles III** since he bought it through the Duchy of Cornwall in 1980. It was previously owned by **Maurice Macmillan,** a Conservative MP and son of former **Prime Minister Harold Macmillan.**

There is a **Highgrove shop** in **Tetbury town centre**. Sometimes coachloads of foreign visitors, upon seeing the shop, imagine that Charles lives above it!

The Highgrove Shop in the centre of Tetbury. Contrary to the belief of some, King Charles III does not live here!

Credit: Cotswolds Tourism/ © Anthony Paul Photography

The 'Perfect Village' and the Yellow Car

Arlington Row at **Arlington** in the **Cotswold village of Bibury** was built in the late **14th century** as a wool store and converted into weavers houses in the late 17th century. It is a Grade I listed building and is owned by the **National Trust**, the heritage conservation charity.

Arlington Row on **Awkward Hill** is a nationally important architectural conservation area depicted on the inside cover of all UK passports issued between 2010-15, alongside the **White Cliffs of Dover** and **Ben Nevis**. It is a popular visitor attraction and probably one of the most photographed Cotswold scenes.

Japanese tourists, in particular, flock to the village, and this is largely attributed to **Emperor Hirohito** having stayed in the village on his European tour when he was a Prince during the first half of the 20th Century. He subsequently became a fervent advocate of the area.

It is believed that **Henry Ford, founder of the Ford Motor Company,** was so taken with Arlington Row that he tried to buy the entire row of cottages so he could dismantle them brick by brick and ship them back to America. Fortunately, this never happened.

The village has been used as a film and television location, most notably for the films Stardust and, according to some, **Bridget Jones's Diary**. In 2017 it was reported that an "ugly" banana yellow car parked by 84-year-old **Peter Maddox** near the cottages had been vandalised, causing £6000 of damage, possibly by visitors who had repeatedly complained that it spoiled photographs. In response, a convoy of 100 bright yellow cars made its way through the village in support of Mr Maddox on 1st April 2017, raising money to help pay his car repair bill.

Arlington Row in Bibury. Credit: Cotswolds Tourism/ © Anthony Paul Photography

England's Favourite House and the Renishaw Boss's Not-So-Favourite House

Eyford House in **Upper Slaughter** was named by the magazine Country Life as **'England's Favourite House'** in 2011. Legend has it that the poet **John Milton** began writing **'Paradise Lost'** in the grounds of the house. The estate was bought by **Merchant Banker Sir Cyril Kleinwort** in 1972 and passed down the generations of his family.

Gloucestershire engineering company **Renishaw**, which was founded in 1973 by **David McMurtry** and **John Deer**, has its headquarters near the market town of **Wotton-under-Edge** and has other bases at **Woodchester** and **Stroud**. In 2000, McMurtry built a **futuristic £30 million mansion** near Wotton-under-Edge, which was featured in the **BBC drama 'Sherlock'** starring **Benedict Cumberbatch**. The tycoon doesn't actually live in the house, because his wife thought it was too flashy.

The Defector's House
Which Returned to the Fold

Sarsden House, in the **village of Sarsden** near **Chipping Norton**, is one of the finest houses in the Cotswolds. It was home to **Shaun Woodward**, MP for **West Oxfordshire** from 1997 to 2001. Elected as a Conservative, he defected to Labour in 1999. Woodward was married to supermarket heiress **Camilla Sainsbury** and was said to be the **only Labour MP with a butler**.

His defection paved the way for a certain **David Cameron** to be elected as MP for the constituency in 2001. Sarsden was sold to property tycoon **Tony Gallagher** in 2006 for **£24 million**. Gallagher hosted **David Cameron's** 50th birthday party at Sarsden in 2016, shortly after he stood down as Prime Minister.

The Countess's Tower

Broadway Tower is an iconic landmark folly on **Broadway Hill**, near the beautiful village of **Broadway**, in **Worcestershire**. It stands at the **second-highest point of the Cotswolds (after Cleeve Hill)**. Broadway Tower's base is 1,024 feet above sea level and the tower itself stands 65 feet tall.

The tower was the brainchild of **Capability Brown** and designed by **James Wyatt** in **1794 in the form of a castle**, and built for the 6th Earl of Coventry as a love token for his wife **Lady Barbara**. It was completed in 1798. The tower was built on a beacon hill, where beacons were lit on special occasions. The tower could be seen from the Earl's two estates in **Worcestershire.**

In 1961, an underground **Royal Observer Corps nuclear bunker** was built 50 yards from the Tower as part of a network of monitoring posts. 15 feet underground, it was staffed continuously from 1961 and was one of the last such **Cold War bunkers** constructed. Although officially decommissioned in 1991, the bunker is now one of the few remaining fully equipped facilities in England. Tours of the bunker are available to the public.

Broadway Tower.

Credit: Cotswolds Tourism/ © Anthony Paul Photography

The Malted Milk Magnate's Manor

These days, **Cowley Manor** in the village of Cowley (between Cheltenham and Cirencester), is an upmarket hotel. The land on which Cowley Manor sits used to belong to the **kings of England**. It was exchanged by Edward the Confessor in return for the land on which he built **Westminster Abbey**. **Sir James Horlick**, the **malted milk magnate**, bought Cowley Manor in the **1890s**. The author **Lewis Carroll** visited Cowley regularly. Local history has it that Carroll wrote his best known book, **Alice in Wonderland**, during his stays in the village, drawing his inspiration from the grounds of Cowley Manor. During the Second World War, Cowley was requisitioned to house the **Cheltenham Ladies College** – as a safe haven from German air attacks.

After the War, Cowley Manor was purchased by **Gloucestershire County Council** and used as offices and an education centre. It fell into something of a decline with most of the original fittings and fixtures in the house and in the garden ripped out or allowed to disintegrate. It was sold to new owners in 1999 who began a painstaking process of restoration to bring it back to its former glory.

In the early 1990s there was a macabre twist to the tale of Cowley Manor, when the **children of Fred and Rosemary West** were placed there by the council's child protection officers. It was there that the children kept mentioning their sister Heather being buried under the patio.

The Poldark House Where Cromwell Stayed

Chavenage House at **Beverston**, near **Tetbury**, has been described as **"the ideal sixteenth-century Cotswold stone manor house"**. It is said to be one of **England's most haunted homes**. One of its former owners, **Nathaniel Stephens**, was a Roundhead supporter and member of **Oliver Cromwell**'s Parliament. Cromwell himself stayed at Chavenage and Stephens supported his **plan to kill the King**, although he was not one of the signatories of **Charles** I's death warrant. He is nevertheless said to have died of remorse soon afterwards. A story is told that on the day of Nathaniel's death, his ghost was seen leaving the house in a coach driven by a **headless coachman** dressed like the hapless king.

In more recent times, Chavenage has been a film location, most famously as **Trenwith House** in 'Poldark'. Perhaps less notably, it was the setting for **'Grace & Favour'**, a spin-off from the department store sitcom **'Are You Being Served'**.

The house is owned by the **Lowsley-Williams** family. **James Lowsley-Williams** is an elite cyclist and presenter on the Global Cycling Network Youtube channel.

The Inspiration for the Houses of Parliament

Toddington Manor at **Toddington, near Tewkesbury**, is described by **Historic England** as **"a very important Gothic-revival building"**. It was designed by gentleman-architect **Charles Hanbury-Tracy**, 1st Baron Sudeley for himself. It is thought to have influenced the designs of both **Highclere Castle (of Downton Abbey fame)** and the **Houses of Parliament.** When the Houses of Parliament were to be rebuilt after the fire in 1834, **Hanbury-Tracy** acted as Chairman of the Commission to choose the new design, and the winning architect, **Charles Barry,** is believed to have adapted his entry to reflect the style exemplified at Toddington.

In 2005 Toddington was purchased by the **artist Damien Hirst** who planned to restore it and use it as a family home and a gallery, both for his own works and for his collection of works by other artists. Since 2006, the house has been covered by what Hirst claims is **the world's biggest span of scaffolding**. At the time of writing, and much to the frustration of locals, restoration work is yet to start in any meaningful way and the manor is still listed on **Historic England's** 'Heritage at Risk' Register.

The 5000 Year-Old Burial Chamber Which Features in a Video Game!

Belas Knap, on **Cleeve Hill** near **Winchcombe,** is a particularly good example of a **Neolithic long barrow,** with a false entrance and side chambers. It is situated along the **Cotswold Way National Trail**.

The name is believed to come from the **Latin word 'bellus' meaning beautiful,** and **'Knap' being the Old English word for the summit of a hill.** The barrow is about 178 feet long, about 60 feet wide and nearly 14 feet high.

At Belas Knap the impressive entrance is a dummy and the burial chambers are entered from the sides of the barrow. When closed and covered by earth they would have been invisible from the outside.

It was probably **constructed around 3000 BC** and was used for successive burials for thousands of years until eventually the burial chambers were deliberately blocked.

Opinion differs as to the reason for the false portal. It may have been to deter grave robbers.

Alternatively, it could be that the false entrance functioned as a 'spirit door', through which the souls of the deceased may walk and receive the offerings left by their descendants during ceremonies.

Although Belas Knap seems in good condition, this is the result of several restorations. **Romano-British pottery** found inside one of the burial chambers show that it was open in Roman times. It was explored between 1863 and 1865 using the archaeological methods of the time, when the **remains of 31 people were found in the chambers**. Four different burial chambers were unearthed, as well as a collection of skeletons from children and one young adult beneath the false entrance. A circle of flat stones was also discovered in the centre of the mound, along with animal bones and flint artefacts. Some years later it was restored by **Mrs Emma Dent of Sudeley Castle**. In 1928–30 the site was excavated again, before being restored as it is today.

Belas Knap features in **'Assassin's Creed Valhalla'**, a 2020 action role-playing video game, which can be played on the Xbox and Playstation. Players need to find the keys in Belas Knap in order to unlock the chest holding **The Morrigan's Guard Light Shield.**

The Eccentric Collector of 22,000 Objects

Snowshill Manor is a National Trust property located in the **village of Snowshill**, Gloucestershire. The Manor fell under the jurisdiction of **Winchcombe Abbey from 821 until the dissolution of monasteries in 1539**. It was then given by **Henry VIII** to his wife at that time, **Catherine Parr**.

It is a sixteenth-century country house, best known for its twentieth-century owner, **Charles Paget Wade**, an eccentric who amassed an enormous collection of objects that interested him because of their colour, craftsmanship and design.

Wade was an architect, artist-craftsman, collector, poet and heir to the family fortune. He restored the property, living in the Priest's House (a small cottage in the garden) and using the Manor house as a home for his collection of objects. By the time of his death **he had amassed over 22,000 objects**. He gave the property and the contents of his collection, which is still housed there, to the National Trust in 1951.

Wade's motto was **"Let nothing perish"**. The collection includes toys, **26 suits of Japanese**

Samurai armour, musical instruments, clocks and more. Today, the main attraction of the house is perhaps the display of Wade's collection.

The Manor is said to be **haunted by a girl in a green dress, a monk, a swordsman** and **Charles Wade himself.**

The Most Complete Set of Stained Glass Windows in England

The Fairford stained glass is a set of 28 pre-Reformation stained glass windows located in **St Mary's Church, Fairford**, Gloucestershire. The medieval stained glass panes are **of national historical and architectural importance** as they constitute what is **"probably the most complete set of medieval stained glass in Britain"** consisting of 28 windows displaying biblical scenes.

The panes were once known as an example of Netherlandish-style glass painting, however they are now attributed to the **Flemish glazier Barnard Flower, glazier to King Henry VII.**

In **1642,** during the Civil War, they **narrowly avoided destruction** when the Roundhead army was marching on the nearby **town of Cirencester**. The windows were hurriedly dismantled and the glass concealed before the troops arrived in the vicinity. During the Second World War, the stained-glass windows were removed and stored in a cellar for safekeeping from 1939 to 1945.

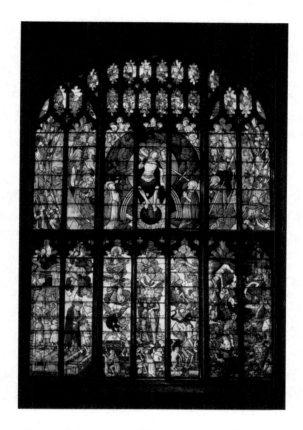

One of the magnificent stained-glass
windows at St Mary's Church, Fairford.

Credit: Cotswolds Tourism/ © Nick Turner Photography

England's Oldest Inn

The **Porch House** in **Stow-on-The-Wold** is said to be the **oldest pub in England**, with timbers that have been carbon dated to approximately **1000 AD**.

It is believed to have been **founded by the Saxon Duke of Cornwall, Athelmar, in 947 AD** and was subsequently run by the **Knights Hospitallers**. It was originally a hospice to shelter lepers, and then an inn, possibly with a dog fighting pit, and eventually a hotel, formerly known as The Royalist. It has also been a family residence and a sweet shop!

The medieval fireplace in the lounge has **'witch's marks'**, which are carvings meant to ward off spells.

The Rollright Stones

The Rollright Stones is the site of **three ancient megalithic monuments, near the village of Long Compton**, on the borders of **Oxfordshire** and **Warwickshire**, on the edge of the **Cotswold hills**. Constructed from local oolitic limestone, the three monuments, now known as **the King's Men** and the **Whispering Knights** in **Oxfordshire** and **the King Stone** in **Warwickshire**, are distinct in their design and purpose. They were built at different periods in late prehistory. The oldest, the Whispering Knights, is **early Neolithic (circa 3,800-3,500 BC)**, the King's Men stone circle is **late Neolithic (circa 2,500 BC)**, and the King Stone is early to **middle Bronze Age (circa 1,500 BC)**. During the period when the three monuments were erected, there was a continuous tradition of ritual behaviour on sacred ground

The Stones take their names from **a legend about a King and his army** who were marching over the Cotswolds when they met a witch who challenged the King saying, "Seven long strides shalt thou take and if Long Compton thou canst see, King of England thou shalt be". On his seventh stride a mound rose up obscuring the view, and the witch turned them all to stone. The King became the King Stone, his army the King's Men and his knights the Whispering Knights (plotting treachery). The witch became an elder tree, supposedly still in the hedge. If it is cut, the spell is broken and the Stones will come back to life.

Legend has it that as the church clock at Great Rollright strikes midnight, the King Stone comes alive. Similarly, the king and his men were said to come to life on certain saints' days.

The Rollright Stones **became associated with fertility** in the late eighteenth and the nineteenth centuries. Several different, related local customs arose in the nineteenth century: **Girls from local villages ran naked around the stones at midnight of Midsummer's Eve** in the belief that they would see the man they would marry. Those who were without children would also pray close to the King Stone. Some even rubbed their bare breasts on the rock to encourage pregnancy.

Pagan groups have made the site home, with many seeking meditation and communion with spirits they believe reside there.

The Rollright Stones.

The Mogul Indian Palace Which Inspired Brighton Pavillion

Sezincote House (pronounced seas in coat), described as **'India in the Cotswolds'** is a **200-year-old Mogul Indian palace** at the centre of a **3500 acre country estate** in Sezincote, near **Moreton-in-Marsh** in Gloucestershire. The estate was bought by **Colonel John Cockerell** in 1795, on his return from Bengal. He died three years later, leaving the estate to his youngest brother, Charles, who had been with him in India in the service of the **East India Company**. Charles employed another brother, **Samuel Pepys Cockerell**, an architect and surveyor to the East India Company, to **build him a house in the Indian manner**. Cockerell had recently built nearby **Daylesford** for **Warren Hastings**, the **first Governor-General of India**.

The house was built in 1805 in the 'Indian Style', **a unique combination of Hindu and Muslim architecture**. It is dominated by its red sandstone colour and features a copper-covered dome, a symbol of heart and heaven, peace and tranquillity. It stands in a romantic landscape of temples, grottoes, waterfalls and canals **reminiscent of the Taj Mahal**. The gardens were designed with the help of Humphrey Repton and are filled with trees and shrubs from around the world. Sezincote is credited with influencing the design of the **Brighton Pavilion** after a visit by The Prince Regent in 1807.

The Monument That Inspired Tolkien

The Four Shire Stone is a 15-foot high monument that marks the place where the **four historic English counties** of **Warwickshire, Oxfordshire, Gloucestershire**, and **Worcestershire** once met. It is on the A44 road, a mile and a half east of **Moreton-in-Marsh**.

Since 1931, with a change to the boundaries of Worcestershire, which saw several parishes absorbed into Gloucestershire, only three of the counties meet at the stone.

Built from local Cotswold stone, probably quarried at nearby Chipping Campden, it is thought to have been built in the mid-1700s, when it replaced an earlier marker stone **dating back to the Middle Ages**. There has been speculation that the **Four Shire Stone inspired** the **'Three Farthing Stone'** in **Tolkien's book 'The Lord of the Rings'.** In that work, the Shire, **the homeland of the hobbits**, is divided into **four farthings, three of which meet at the 'Three Farthing Stone'.**

It has not always been well-cared for. It was once a convenient venue for prize fights, where pugilists (boxers) could evade prosecution in one county by hopping across the border to another. It was even demolished by a wayward lorry in 1955! The poor state of the stone inspired **James Hayman-Joyce**, a local semi-retired chartered surveyor, to form the Four Shire Stone Restoration Committee with the aim of raising £20,000 to restore the Four Shire Stone to its former glory. The project comprises restoring and repairing the stonework, replacing the railings and enhancing the engravings on all four sides of the pillar. The work was completed in October 2022.

Tolkien was a frequent visitor to Moreton-in-Marsh, and was particularly fond of a pint of beer in The Bell Inn. **The Bell Inn** is acknowledged to be Tolkien's inspiration for **The Prancing Pony pub** from his books. A branch of the Tolkien Society awarded the pub with a blue plaque to commemorate the link.

JRR Tolkien liked to visit **Chipping Campden** too. His personal letters show that he stayed at **The Red Lion Inn** many times with his son Michael. He also signed a copy of The Lord of the Rings for the pub's landlord back in the 1950s.

The Nuclear Bunker Ready for the Prime Minister!

At **Ullenwood**, near Cheltenham, there is **an extensive underground nuclear bunker** which was built in the 1950s in response to escalating tensions between the **USA and Soviet Russia during the Cold War**. It lies just to the **west of Leckhampton Hill** and is on the site of the former **Ullenwood army camp** which was used during the two World Wars as a US military hospital.

After the wars, the camp was kept by the War Office for civil defence purposes, and the bunker was built to provide a safe location for local government at the height of the Cold War.

In 1963 it was bought by Gloucestershire County Council and in more recent years the Gloucestershire Fire & Rescue Service have used it for training exercises. The Council put the bunker and its 2.2 hectare site up for auction in 2002 but it failed to make the reserve of £400,000.

The following year the property was bought by a local businessman who has since built a detached house in the grounds, leaving the bunker undisturbed.

The bunker is two floors deep - although there are rumours of a lower floor that's been sealed off. It covers almost 1300 square metres, and has **concrete walls more than two feet thick.**

In the heart of the bunker is the map room with an observation balcony from which in-coming Russian bombers would have been logged and anti-aircraft defences co-ordinated.

Designed to be self-sufficient in the event of an attack, the bunker was **hermetically sealed to prevent radiation poisoning** and had its own water supply, generator, more than three dozen phone lines and ample storage space for provisions.

Secret government documents released by the National Archives in 2005 revealed contingency plans in the event of a nuclear attack which included **scrambling the Prime Minister to the bunker at Ullenwood**.

Trouble in Tetbury

The Trouble House pub and restaurant in **Tetbury** is rumoured to have frequently lived up to its name.

Around 1754 a Tetbury carpenter named **John Reeve** built a pub at this location, which was known as 'troublesome' at that time due to its poor quality and habit of flooding.

Two early landlords – **John Bird** (1757) and **Richard Reeve** (1768) – were the first to suffer a bit of bad luck at the Trouble House. John Bird lost 'several' wives who died young and Richard Reeve (son of the original builder John Reeve) hit a sticky patch financially when many of his male regulars were forcibly abducted by His Majesty's press gangs to **fight in the American Revolution.**

The pub was caught up in the **agricultural riots of 1830** as local farm labourers vented their displeasure at the introduction of mechanical haymaking and threshing machines. An unlucky farmer transporting a new piece of machinery hidden in a laden hay wagon was spotted in Tetbury and chased by an angry mob who surrounded the wagon outside the Trouble House and set fire to it.

There are claims that in the later 1800s the Trouble House's financial fortunes suffered a downturn and the pub fell into disrepair. Tradition holds that an owner at this time embarked on a refurbishment which bankrupted him so he hung himself from a beam in the pub in despair. The half-reconstructed building was taken over by another innkeeper who also fell on hard times and drowned himself in a nearby pond. Eventually the pub was purchased by a wealthy local businessman who finished the repairs, replacing the thatched roof with Cotswold tiles and re-naming it the **'Trouble House'** in honour of its tragic history.

In 1931 the pub was purchased by a Bristol businessman **Frank Wills**, who made some major renovations incorporating the stables into the main pub. It was at this time that the **Trouble House ghost**, the **'Lady in Blue'**, began to make a nuisance of herself. She is rumoured to appear as a very life-like woman with long dark hair (occasionally wearing a hood) in the back-rooms of the pub and likes to move things around.

The Birthplace of Croquet

Chastleton House at **Chastleton, Oxfordshire,** near **Moreton-in-Marsh**, is now owned by the National Trust. It has two croquet lawns, originally laid out by **Walter Whitmore-Jones** in the 1860s. **His version of the rules of croquet published in The Field in 1865 became definitive**, and Chastleton is considered the **birthplace of croquet** as a competitive sport.

The house is famous for an episode from the **English Civil War** in which a loyal wife duped and drugged Roundhead soldiers to save her husband. At the end of the **Battle of Worcester**, **Royalist Arthur Jones** fled back to Chastleton, closely followed by Roundhead soldiers who were searching the area for fugitives. Arthur had managed to hide in a closet but his horse had given away his presence and the soldiers decided to stay the night and continue the search the following day. Unfortunately the soldiers decided to sleep in the first bedchamber they came to, which was a room in the south-west corner of the house, off of which was the closet where Arthur was hiding (now known as the Cavalier Room). Arthur's wife Sarah brought opium-laced ale for the soldiers to drink, allowing Arthur to slip out of the room and take a fresh horse to make his escape.

2 - HISTORY

Burford's Apparition with a Fiery Coach

Burford Priory, in the **Cotswold town of Burford**, is on the site of a **13th-century Augustinian hospital,** and is now an **Elizabethan** private house. It has been owned by 17th century Speaker of the House of Commons, **William Lenthall** and, more recently, **Rupert Murdoch's daughter Elisabeth** and her former husband **Matthew Freud.**

The house was built by judge and local landowner **Sir Lawrence Tanfield**. He and his second wife **Elizabeth Evans** had a reputation for corruption and for being notoriously harsh to their tenants. **Local legend tells of a fiery coach** containing Tanfield and his wife flying around the town and bringing a curse upon all who see it. It has been speculated that the apparition may have been caused by a **local tradition of burning effigies of the unpopular couple** that began after their deaths. The visitations apparently ended when **local clergymen trapped Lady Tanfield's ghost in a corked glass bottle** during an exorcism and **threw it into the River Windrush**. During droughts locals would fill the river from buckets to ensure that the bottle did not rise above the surface and free the spirit.

Other apparitions at the **Priory itself include a brown monk** and the **ghost of an old-fashioned gamekeeper** carrying a blunderbuss or flintlock pistol, who was wrongly executed for the murder of a servant in the late 17th century.

The Burial Place of Henry VIII's Wife

Sudeley Castle, near **Winchcombe**, is the **only private castle in England to have a queen buried within the grounds** - **Queen Katherine Parr**, the **last and surviving wife of King Henry VIII** – who lived and died in the castle.

King Charles I found refuge at Sudeley during the Civil War, when his **nephew Prince Rupert** established headquarters at the Castle. Following its 'slighting' on Cromwell's orders at the end of the Civil War, Sudeley lay neglected and derelict for nearly 200 years before being rescued in 1837 by the wealthy Worcester glove-makers, brothers **John and William Dent**. Their descendants still live at Sudeley today.

Actress and model Liz Hurley married Indian textile heir Arun Nayar at the Castle in 2007. They divorced in 2011. Hurley is a friend of the current part-owner of Sudeley, **Henry Dent-Brocklehurst**, who is **Godson to Camilla, the Queen Consort.**

Liz Hurley was a Cotswolds resident between 2002-2015, when she **sold her home just outside the village of Barnsley for a cool £9 million.**

The First King of England and the Naked Gardener

Abbey House Manor at **Malmesbury** dates from the 1500s, but was built on 13th-century foundations, and there are records of buildings on the site as early as the 11th century. The house's history stretches back even further still.

Monks working at **Malmesbury Abbey** would have lived there, at a time when the Abbey was one of the leading European seats of learning. **The first 'King of all England', Aethelstan**, was **buried in Malmesbury Abbey in 939 AD**. His remains were lost during the Reformation and are **rumoured to be in the gardens at Abbey House**. His empty tomb is at Malmesbury Abbey.

Today, the five acres of stunning gardens are, at times, open to the public. They were created by the late **Ian Douglas Pollard**, known as the **'Naked Gardener'**, due to his penchant for working in the nude.

Churchill's Birthplace

Blenheim Palace in **Woodstock**, Oxfordshire, is the seat of the **Dukes of Marlborough** and the only non-royal, non-episcopal country house in England to hold the title of palace.   It was **designated a UNESCO World Heritage Site in 1987.**

Blenheim has 200 rooms and 1000 windows. When it was first built, the size of the window was determined in relation to the importance of the person who lived in that room. Servants had smaller windows and members of the Duke and Duchess' family had large windows.

Winston Churchill's father, Lord Randolph Churchill is a **descendant of the 1st Duke of Marlborough, John Churchill**. It was **at Blenheim Palace on the 30th November 1874 at 1.30am** that the **wartime Prime Minister**, considered by many to be the **'Greatest Briton of all time'**, was born. Typical of the impatience that he was to demonstrate in later life, he arrived unexpectedly two months early. **Churchill spent much time at Blenheim** as a child and **is buried at St Martin's Churchyard in Bladon, Oxfordshire, just outside the Blenheim Palace grounds.**

Blenheim Palace.

The Cotswold Wool Trade

According to a 12th Century saying, **'in Europe the best wool is English and in England the best wool is Cotswold'**. The **'Golden Fleece'** obtained from the **golden, long-haired Cotswold Lion breed**, thought to be **introduced by the Romans during their invasion of our British Isles**, was renowned for its heavy wool clip. The wool, from a million medieval sheep on the Cotswolds, was extremely high-quality and a profitable European export. Italian merchants, in particular, clamoured to buy wool from the Cotswolds.

As a result of the flourishing wool trade, **the Cotswolds accrued a great wealth**, and the impact of this wealth can still be seen to this day. Many towns and villages in the Cotswolds are home to **'wool churches'** - that is, churches which were built or enlarged by the local wool merchants. These devout merchants adorned their churches in **hope of securing a spot in heaven**. The churches typically feature Gothic characteristics - the favoured architectural style of the time - such as imposing towers, large stained-glass windows, menacing gargoyles and decorative interiors. **The Church of St. John the Baptist in Cirencester, St. James' Church in Chipping Campden and St. Peter's Church in Winchcombe are some of**

the finest examples. The merchants also built themselves magnificent homes, many of which can still be seen today.

Wool production in the Cotswolds went into decline between 1750 and 1850. By the end of the First World War, only a few flocks of the Cotswold Lion remained and it had become a rare breed.

The Cotswold Lion is now expanding again, thanks both to rare breed conservationists and a demand for sheep with high growth rate. Farmer and television presenter **Adam Henson** has described it as "a big, docile breed that is easy to work with and is certainly one of my favourites". There are now more than 50 flocks and about 3,000 animals around the UK, many of them in the Cotswolds.

The Amphitheatre
for 8000 People

In **Roman Britain, Cirencester was known as Corinium Dobunnorum**, and was the **second biggest town in Britannia, after Londinium (London)** with a population of over 10,000. Its **amphitheatre**, the site of which can still be visited today, is estimated to have been **built in the 2nd century**. It is also the **second largest** in Roman Britain, indicating the significance of the location in Roman times. The amphitheatre could **hold about 8,000 spectators**.

Archaeological digs have uncovered the earthworks, revealing the outline of the construction, which is still visible. The banking reaches 25 feet from the bottom of the arena and the arena itself is approximately 150 feet by 135 feet. Roman artefacts including coins and pottery have been discovered on the site. After the Roman army left Britain, it was fortified against Saxon invaders, but in AD 577 a stronghold believed to be Cirencester is reported as falling to the Saxons and the amphitheatre then remained abandoned for several centuries.

In the Middle Ages the **Abbot of Cirencester enclosed it for use as a rabbit warren**. Its local name, **the Bull Ring**, suggests that it **may once have been used for bull-baiting** - a return to its original purpose.

The amphitheatre, which is now owned by English Heritage and managed by Cirencester Town Council, is cut off from Cirencester town centre by a dual carriageway. Various proposals have been made in recent times to improve links to the town centre and make better use of the site, but at the time of writing none of the proposals had been implemented.

The Roman Villa Found When Digging for a Ferret!

Chedworth Roman Villa is located **near the Cotswold village of Chedworth** and is a scheduled monument. It is **one of the largest and most elaborate Roman villas so far discovered in Britain** and one with the latest occupation beyond the Roman period. The villa was built in phases from the **early 2nd century to the 5th century.** The villa was accidentally **discovered in 1864 by Thomas Margetts**, a **gamekeeper who was digging for a ferret** and instead **found fragments of mosaic.** In 1924 the villa was **acquired by the National Trust** who have conducted a long-term conservation programme, with new on-site facilities and cover-buildings.

The Finest Collection of Roman Objects from a Town

Cirencester's Corinium Museum is **home to the finest and most extensive Romano-British collection of objects ever** discovered from a particular town. The Roman town of Corinium, now known as Cirencester, was established shortly after the Roman conquest of Britain. It was the territory of the friendly tribe of the Dobunni and was **the largest town outside London.**

The museum is particularly famous for its intact Roman mosaics, including the Hare mosaic, which has **inspired modern-day Cirencester to adopt the hare as its unofficial emblem.**

Other notable exhibits include two gravestones of **Roman legionaries**, part of the **Jupiter Column from the town's Roman Forum**, **Saxon jewellery** and a **Civil War coin hoard.**

Cirencester had an Abbey

The Abbey Grounds open space in Cirencester town centre contains the site of **St Mary's Abbey**. The abbey was **founded by Henry I around AD 1117**, on the **site of a Saxon church** which **in turn stood on the site of a Roman church** and was consecrated in 1176 in the presence of **Henry II**. The abbot became Lord of the Manor of Cirencester, and was granted the right to hold wool fairs. The abbey prospered, much to the annoyance of the townsfolk, who felt that the abbot exercised too much authority. Conflict between the townsfolk and monks continued throughout the medieval period.

Originally, apart from the abbey buildings of church, cloisters and various residences for the Abbot, canons and lay brothers, there were two sets of farm buildings. The lake which can be seen today was the trout lake for the abbey. The rest of the grounds were used as gardens and to grow food for the abbey. Until 1963 some of the old farm and abbey buildings were still present, but these were removed to make way for the housing seen today.

The south porch of the **St John Baptist Church**, which can be seen on the Market Place today, was built by Cirencester Abbey around 1480 and only connected to the church in the 18th century. The St John Baptist Church is **believed to be the second largest Parish Church in England.**

The Last Battle of the Civil War

The Battle of Stow fought on 21st March, **1646** was **the last major battle of the First Civil War**, which ultimately **led to the execution of King Charles I** and **laid the foundation of our parliamentary democracy.**

The Royalist forces spent the night before the battle on a hill at **Donnington**, about 1 ½ miles north of Stow. **A stone obelisk on a public footpath today marks this spot.** The Parliamentarian forces attacked the hill. After being driven back by the Royalists, a second Parliamentary advance followed and this time the Royalist forces were pushed back in the direction of Stow.

Over **200 Royalists were slaughtered** in the Market Square and **1500 were imprisoned in St Edward's Church** overnight. The street leading from the Market Square became **Digbeth Street**, meaning **'Duck's Bath'** because there was so much blood running through the street that ducks could bathe in it. Today a simple stone stands in the churchyard of St Edward's Church to honour the men who fought and died.

THE ENGLISH CIVIL WAR
BATTLE OF STOW 21ST MARCH 1646

NEAR THIS CROSS SIR JACOB ASTLEY SURRENDERED TO PARLIAMENTARY FORCES FOLLOWING DEFEAT AT THE BATTLE OF STOW. SOME 200 ROYALISTS WERE SLAUGHTERED IN THE SQUARE AND 1500 IMPRISONED IN THE CHURCH OVERNIGHT. THIS WAS THE FINAL BATTLE OF THE FIRST CIVIL WAR LEADING TO THE END OF THE ROYALIST OCCUPATION OF OXFORD.

STOW AND DISTRICT CIVIC SOCIETY

A plaque in Stow-on-the-Wold town centre,
marking its role in the Civil War.

Credit: Cotswolds Tourism/ © Anthony Paul Photography

The Blood of Christ or an 'Unctuous Gum'?

Hailes Abbey, near **Winchcombe**, was **founded by the Earl of Cornwall in 1246.** While in Germany in 1268, the **Earl's son Edmund obtained what was believed to be a portion of the blood shed by Christ on the Cross – the Holy Blood.**

Edmund **presented a portion of the blood relic to Hailes**. Great ceremonies accompanied the arrival of the relic at the abbey on 14 September 1270, **the Feast of the Holy Cross.**

The **Holy Blood** was first housed in a temporary shrine but then an entirely new east end to the church was constructed on a magnificent scale. The design was believed to be inspired by **Henry III**'s rebuilding of Westminster Abbey.

The relic immediately **became a focus of pilgrimage**. It was believed that the relic would only be visible to people whose sins had been forgiven after confession and penance. This attracted pilgrims who were worried that they remained in a state of sin after confession.

When **Henry VIII** started to reform what he

saw as **the abuses within the Catholic Church** – particularly the financial gains made from holy relics – **Hailes Abbey was soon in the sights of the evangelical reformers**. According to one source, **Anne Boleyn** sent some of her chaplains to enquire into the 'abomynable abuse' of pilgrimage to Hailes. Three years later, **the relic was denounced during a sermon outside St Paul's Cathedral in London as being nothing more than duck's blood**. Commissioners including the **Bishop of Worcester** were dispatched to Hailes to examine the relic. After pronouncing it to be **not blood but an 'unctuous gum'**, they sealed it in a box and took it with them to London.

The shrine of the Holy Blood was stripped of its precious metal and jewelled adornment and then dismantled. Soon after, Hailes fell victim to Henry VIII's Suppression of the Monasteries and the church was reduced to ruins.

The Vicar and the Precursor to Aspirin

Edward Stone, a vicar from **Chipping Norton in Oxfordshire**, is generally recognised as the man who gave the first scientific description of the effects of **willow bark**.

In 1757, he had 'accidentally' tasted willow bark and noted its extreme bitterness and its resemblance to Peruvian bark. He experimented by gathering willow bark from pollarded willows, dried it for more than three months in a bag on the outside of a baker's oven, pounded and sifted it. He dosed himself, using tiny amounts and then increased the dose. Stone gave powdered willow bark over several years to about 50 of his parishioners who were complaining of fevers and it was successful in many of them. When fevers failed to respond to willow bark, he added quinine, which he found more effective. Thus, **Stone had accidentally discovered a source of salicylate, the precursor of aspirin.**

In 1763 he wrote a letter to the **Earl of Macclesfield**, then **President of the Royal Society in London**, in which he describes treating patients suffering from ague (fever) with 20 grains (approximately a gram) of powdered willow bark in a dram of water every four hours. Stone's interest in willows was due to the ancient 'Doctrine of Signatures' - the age-old belief that plants resemble the very body parts they are intended to treat.

William Morris and the Arts & Crafts Movement

William Morris (1834-1898), was a **founder of the British Arts and Crafts movement**, and sought to restore the prestige and methods of hand-made crafts, including textiles, in opposition to the 19th century tendency toward factory-produced textiles. He created his own workshop and designed dozens of patterns for hand-produced woven and printed cloth, upholstery and other textiles.

Morris believed passionately in the importance of **creating beautiful, well-made objects that could be used in everyday life**, and that were produced in a way that allowed their makers to remain connected both with their product and with other people. His ideas were hugely influential to the generation of decorative artists.

He is often remembered by his most famous quote: **"Have nothing in your house that you do not know to be useful or believe to be beautiful."**

The summer home of William Morris, **Kelmscott Manor, is a Grade I listed farmhouse**, built around 1570 adjacent to the River Thames, near Lechlade. William Morris chose it as his summer home, signing a joint lease with the Pre-Raphaelite painter **Dante Gabriel Rossetti** in the summer of 1871.

Morris loved the house as a work of true craftsmanship, totally unspoilt and unaltered, and in harmony with the village and the surrounding countryside. He considered it so natural in its setting as to be almost organic, it looked to him as if it had "grown up out of the soil".

Its beautiful gardens, with barns, dovecote, a meadow and stream, provided a constant source of inspiration. The house contains an outstanding collection of the possessions and works of Morris, his family and his Arts & Crafts associates, including furniture, original textiles, pictures, carpets, ceramics and metalwork. It reopened to the public in March 2022 following a £6 million restoration project.

The Space Shuttle
Came to Fairford

The NASA Space Shuttle landed at RAF Fairford in May 1983 en route from the Paris Air Show, although it was on the back of a Jumbo Jet at the time.

The two-mile long runway at RAF Fairford was the UK's only TransOceanic Abort Landing site for the Shuttle, and one of only four in western Europe.

That meant that whenever the Shuttle launched, depending on the launch and flight path, **a team of NASA experts were on hand at the air base in case the Shuttle crew had to abort its mission** minutes after take-off.

The European landing sites (the others are in France and Spain) would only have been needed if problems occurred in a specific window between two and a half minutes and eight and a half minutes after take-off, when the Shuttle would have gone too far to be able to turn around and land back in Florida but had not gone far enough to continue up into space or fly around the world once.

If the Shuttle had landed in the Cotswolds, it would have triggered two huge sonic booms as its nose and tail broke through the atmosphere.

Concorde's Test Flight Landed at Fairford

Chief Test Pilot Brian Trubshaw and his **co-pilot John Cochrane** took the controls of the **first British-built Concorde plane** and made the **momentous 22-minute flight between Filton in Bristol and RAF Fairford in Gloucestershire** on 9th April 1969. The normally press-shy Trubshaw concluded that the trip was 'wizard – a cool, calm and collected operation'. This was despite two radio altimeters failing mid-air. After a slight bounce, he made a successful landing to the relief of nervous onlookers.

The Minister of Technology at the time, Labour's **Tony Benn**, was impressed and **called the aircraft a 'beautiful bird'.** The New York Times was less enamoured, **labelling it 'an ungainly goose'.**

Les Slade of Cirencester breached security to get pictures of the landing at Fairford. In 2003, a historic photograph taken of Concorde touching down after its maiden UK flight in 1969 went to auction. It was signed by both Trubshaw and Cochrane.

3 - BUSINESS

George At Home

Fashion tycoon **George Davies**, who **built the Next empire** and **created both the Per Una brand at M&S and George at Asda**, lives near **Moreton-in-Marsh** and runs his businesses from premises locally. He is reported to have a fleet of luxury cars and a **private jet which has been kept at Gloucestershire Airport**. The brands created by Davies are said to account for **18% of the High Street and have contributed £72 billion to the womenswear market.**

Diddly Squat

Former Top Gear Presenter, Jeremy Clarkson's farm, Diddly Squat, in the **village of Chadlington, near Chipping Norton**, has become well known since the launch of the **'Clarkson's Farm'** video series on **Amazon Prime** in June 2021. **Diddly Squat has a popular farm shop** which sells locally-produced goods, including **Clarkson's own Hawkstone beer**, as well as **milk (branded as 'Cow Juice')** and **honey (labelled 'Bee Juice')**. In August 2022, Clarkson was ordered to shut the farm's cafe and restaurant after the local council claimed it had breached planning rules. At the time of writing, Clarkson had launched an appeal against the decision.

The JCB Tycoon and the £50 Jar of Honey

JCB digger tycoon **Lord Anthony Bamford** has an estate, **Daylesford**, in the Cotswolds **near Kingham**. The estate was **the venue for Prime Minister Boris Johnson's wedding party**, which was **delayed because of the Covid pandemic, in 2022**. **Anthony's wife, Lady Carole Bamford**, founded the upmarket **Daylesford Organic farmshop** on the estate. It also has two shops in London. The business supplied £27,000 worth of organic takeaway food to Boris Johnson at Downing Street during the pandemic. Their produce can be a bit pricey - an 800g jar of honey from the estate costs £50 (2022 prices).

Europe's Largest Aeroplane Graveyard

Cotswold Airport, formerly **RAF Kemble**, was the **home to the Red Arrows until 1983**. The airport, now privately-owned, is **known as 'Europe's largest aeroplane graveyard'** as it is **home to Air Salvage International**, who dismantle 50-60 passenger jets at the end of their life each year, into more than 2000 parts. Once they **found £4 million of cocaine stashed behind a toilet panel!**

The Training College With its Own Motorway

The M96 is a four-lane, **400m long stretch of motorway** at the **Fire Service College** in the **Cotswold town of Moreton-in-Marsh**, now **owned by outsourcing giant Capita.** It is **used to train emergency service workers in how to deal with major traffic incidents.**

The motorway at the Fire Service College, Moreton-in-Marsh.

Credit: Capita

The Exclusive Private Members Club

Close to **David and Victoria Beckham's** home, **set in 100 acres,** is the **exclusive Soho Farmhouse private members club** where **Meghan Markle held her hen party.** The retreat opened in 2015 and comprises 40 cabins, a seven-bedroom farmhouse and a four-bedroom cottage. Guests can use bicycles to travel between the dining venues, a 55-seat art deco-style cinema and a boating lake.

Prince Harry and Meghan were regular visitors before moving to California. Other visitors include **actors Liv Tyler** and **Eddie Redmayne** and **model Cara Delavigne.**

The Home-Grown £150 Billion Company

Wealth management firm **St James's Place,** which is part of the FTSE100 index of the UK's biggest companies, was **founded in Cirencester** and still has its headquarters in the town. The business was founded by **Mike Wilson CBE, Sir Mark Weinberg** and **Lord Rothschild** in 1991 as **J Rothschild Assurance** and now **has around £150 billion of funds under management.**

The Cotswold-Born Price Comparison Website

The **money.co.uk** price comparison website was launched by **Cotswolds entrepreneur Chris Morling** in 2008.   In 2015 it was ranked as having the second fastest growing profits of the top 100 private companies in Britain. The company previously had its head office in the 150-year-old **Cecily Hill Barracks**, a former British Army barracks in Cirencester, **known locally as 'The Castle'**. Following a £3 million renovation of 'The Castle', with the interior design done by **Laurence Llewelyn-Bowen**, the company received huge press coverage. **The business was sold for £140 million to ZPG plc, the company behind property website Zoopla, in 2017.**

The National Pub
of the Year

The Frogmill Inn and Hotel at **Shipton Oliffe**, Andoversford was owned by **world-famous chef Marco Pierre White**. The chef owned The Frogmill from August 2013 until it was forced to shut in 2016 as nine of his firms went into administration. The **16th century, Grade II listed building**, which features a classic Cotswold golden limestone façade, was **taken over by family-run chain Brakspear** who have 130 pubs across the UK and underwent a £3.5 million refurbishment before reopening in July 2018. It was **named Pub of the Year in the National Pub and Bar Awards 2022**.

The First Agricultural College in the English-Speaking World

The **Royal Agricultural University (RAU)** in Cirencester was **established in 1845** and **was the first agricultural college in the English-speaking world. The King, when he was Prince Charles, became its Patron in 1982**, following a long line of monarchs to hold the role, **starting with Queen Victoria.** Its alumni include television presenter **Jonathan Dimbleby, former Secretary of State for Wales Simon Hart, former Environment Minister Richard (now Lord) Benyon, Cotswolds MP Sir Geoffrey Clifton-Brown** and **racehorse trainers Henry Cecil** and **Nicky Henderson.**

The Polo Club Where Charles Courted Controversy

Cirencester Polo Club is situated at **Ivy Lodge** on the **Cirencester Park estate of the Bathurst family**. It was founded in 1894 by the 7th Earl Bathurst. **King Edward VIII** played at the club, as have **King Charles III** and **his sons, Princes William and Harry**. It was here that Prince Charles, as he was, caused controversy in 2009 by **calling Club Chairman Kuldip Singh Dhillon by his nickname of 'Sooty'**, prompting accusations of racism, although **Dhillon himself was not remotely offended and described it as a 'term of affection'**.

The other main polo club in the area is the **Beaufort Polo Club,** near **Westonbirt Arboretum, owned by the Tomlinson family,** where Charles, William and Harry have also played.

The Games Company Who Flew Above 'Angry Birds'

Based in **The Old Museum** in **Cirencester, computer games company Neon Play** was **founded by Cotswolds entrepreneur Oli Christie.** Their game **'Flick Football'** briefly went above **'Angry Birds'** in the games charts. Another of their games, **'Paper Glider'** became **Apple's 10 billionth app download.** Their game **Roller Splat** has had **over 60m downloads** and **topped the charts in over 80 countries. Neon Play became the first UK mobile games company to win the Queen's Award for Innovation in 2013.** Oli Christie launched the 'Rock The Cotswolds' campaign in 2013 to change perceptions and portray a 'cool' image of the Cotswolds in order to attract more young professionals to the area. He was made a **Deputy Lieutenant for Gloucestershire in 2017.**

No Business Like
Snow Business

Snow Business, based in an 18th-century watermill in Stroud (now called the **Snow Mill!**), produces over **160 different types of artificial snow** as well as frost, ice, snowballs, snowmen, icicles, igloos and icebergs. The company has **worked on films** including **Band of Brothers, Die Another Day, Golden Eye, The Day After Tomorrow**, the **Harry Potter** series, **The Lion, the Witch and the Wardrobe, The Muppet Christmas Carol** and **The Golden Compass.**

On 23rd November 2006, Snow Business International **set a Guinness World Record for the largest area covered with continuously falling artificial snow**, covering the **New Bond Street, Bond Street and Old Bond Street areas of London simultaneously,** using an **eco-friendly snow made from seaweed**. The area measured 12,462.78 m2.

In 1996 the company was tasked with covering over 100 acres with artificial snow to create the epic setting for the **Prince of Denmark's monologue in Kenneth Brannagh's Hamlet.**

4. THE GREAT OUTDOORS

Painswick Church's
99 Yew Trees

The **churchyard of St Mary's Church** in the **Cotswold village of Painswick** was described by the renowned historian **Alec Clifton-Taylor** as **"the grandest churchyard in England"** with its famous tombs and yew trees.

Legend suggests that **there are just 99 yew trees growing in Painswick churchyard and that the devil would destroy the hundredth if it were ever planted**. The yew trees were all planted in the early 1700s and when they are counted, some get the figure to more than 100, but no two people get the same answer!

In the year 2000 St Mary's was faced with a dilemma. Every parish in the Diocese of Gloucester was given a yew tree to plant to mark the millennium. Painswick was chosen to host a special service when all the young yew trees were blessed and given out.

Parish officials bravely planted the 100th yew on the north side of the church. Contrary to the legend, it is doing well.

The Yew Trees at St Mary's Church, Painswick.
Credit: Cotswolds Tourism/ © Nick Turner Photography

One of the lakes, surrounded by holiday homes, at Cotswold Water Park. Credit: Cotswolds Tourism

180 Lakes Made from Quarrying

The **Cotswold Water Park** is the **United Kingdom's largest marl (lime-rich) lake system**, straddling the Wiltshire-Gloucestershire border, northwest of Cricklade and south of Cirencester, covering 14 Cotswold villages. **There are over 180 lakes, spread over 42 square miles**

The park is a mix of nature conservation activities, including nature reserves; recreation, including sailing, fishing, a country park and beach with water sports and play areas, rural villages and holiday accommodation. The area **attracts over 500,000 visitors a year.** It is a significant area for wildlife and particularly for wintering and breeding birds.

The lakes were created in the second half of the 20th century by large-scale extraction of limestone gravel. The Water Park is the location of a number of developments of holiday homes, some of which can cost several millions of pounds. In 2021, **177 of the Water Park's lakes were designated a Site of Special Scientific Interest (SSSI).** According to Natural England, it was unusual for a "completely man-made site" to become an SSSI.

The Source of The Thames

The **source of the River Thames** is disputed. **The Environment Agency**, the **Ordnance Survey** and other authorities have the **source of the river as being The Thames Head at Trewsbury Mead** near the **village of Coates**, just outside Cirencester.

Others contend that the true source of the **Thames is at Seven Springs**, some 11 miles further north, and east of Gloucester.

Cotswold Stone

The Cotswolds is famous for its **honey-coloured chocolate box villages, dry stone walls** and **imposing wool churches**, all of which are made from the same building material, **Cotswold stone.**

Cotswold stone is a **yellow Oolitic Jurassic Limestone, formed between 206 and 144 million years ago** when the area that is now the Cotswolds **was then covered in a warm sea.** It was created by layer upon layer of shell fragments building up over time on the bottom of the warm seabed. **The colour of the stone changes slightly as you move through the Cotswolds, being honey coloured in the north, golden in the central Cotswolds and progressing to a pearly white in Bath in the south of the region.**

Due to the abundance of the stone and its soft easy to carve nature, **Cotswold stone has been a popular building material since the middle ages and still is to this day.** In a Cotswold house, almost everything is constructed from the stone, including the roof tiles. Certain quarries were singled out for major projects. From Taynton, near Burford, **large quantities of creamy stone were transported to Oxford for use on its colleges** and later in the **construction of Eton College, Windsor**

Castle and **Blenheim Palace**. The quarries at Corsham supplied the stone used in the **construction of Bath**, whilst stone from Minchinhampton was used for the **Houses of Parliament** and material from Leckhampton was **used to build Cheltenham**.

Another feature of the Cotswolds is the **dry stone wall**. As **no cement or earth is used in the making of dry stone walls**, the air can get through and the wall remains dry meaning that a **properly built wall can last many hundreds of years** with very little attention. It is said that **the network of dry stone walls in The Cotswolds is at least the same length as the Great Wall of China!**

Colesbourne Park
Snowdrops

The **snowdrop collection** at **Colesbourne Park** originated in the plantings made by **Henry John Elwes** (1846-1922). The estate has been in the Elwes family since it was purchased in 1789 by John Elwes, son of the **celebrated miser John Elwes**, who is **believed to be one of the models for the character of Ebenezer Scrooge** in **Charles Dickens' 'A Christmas Carol'. Another inspiration for Scrooge was Jemmy Wood, the miserly banker from nearby Gloucester.**

The main house on the estate was **requisitioned during the Second World War by the Gloster Aircraft Company**, where they worked on the **design of Britain's first jet aircraft, the Gloster Meteor.**

In 1874, Henry Elwes **discovered Galanthus elwesiis whilst travelling in western Turkey** and he became one of the **prominent galanthophiles (snowdrop collectors)** of his day. It is clear that he planted widely, as the Colesbourne Park garden today contains large populations of snowdrops, many of them hybrids, descended from those plantings.

New varieties have been added to the collection each year, with **the collection now totalling over 300 different types.** The Gardens are **regarded as one of the best snowdrop displays to visit in England.** The Gardens include **an arboretum of rare trees collected over 120 years, many of which are 'Champion trees' listed in the Tree Register of the British Isles,** and a natural blue lagoon. **The topaz blue colour of the water is created by a special clay** that travels down the valleys to the lagoon, creating an azure oasis.

The Gardens Recreated from a 200-Year-Old Painting

The **Painswick Rococo Garden**, as it is known today, **only exists thanks to a painting from 1748.**

The word **'rococo' describes a period of art that was fashionable in Europe in the 1700s,** characterised by ornamental decoration, the use of pastel colours and asymmetry. In England, in the 1700s, the upper middle classes loved to show off their wealth by indulging in the flamboyant and the frivolous, and their gardens became an elaborate playroom where they would entertain and party.

The **grounds of Painswick House, including the Rococo Garden, were laid out by Benjamin Hyett II (1708-62) (brother of Nicholas Hyett, constable and keeper of the Castle of Gloucester)** in the 1740s.

Benjamin Hyett asked **Thomas Robins the Elder** to **paint the garden in 1748**. The garden was abandoned in the 1950s and was a jungle by 1980. **Painswick House's owner, Lord Dickinson**, who inherited the house in 1955, was inspired to restore the gardens after reading an article about their history in 1984. **Thomas Robins's painting provided the blueprint for the garden to be restored**. The garden includes woodland, flower and vegetable plots, garden buildings and a maze. Several varieties of snowdrop are found in the grounds. There are a series of ponds and streams with small waterfalls.

The garden is the only surviving example of the rococo period which is open to the public.

Exotic Trees are a Growing Attraction

The **Cotswolds has two famous arboreta** - **Westonbirt** and **Batsford**.

The **National Arboretum at Westonbirt, near Tetbury, comprises some 15,000 trees and shrubs, with 2,500 species of tree from all over the world, covering an area of approximately 600 acres.** The Old Arboretum hosts exotic trees from across the globe dating back to the 1850s. It is now owned and run by Forestry England.

Batsford Arboretum,near Moreton-in-Marsh, is a 55-acre arboretum and botanical garden with around 2,900 trees, including a large collection of Japanese maples, magnolias and pines.

The estate of Batsford Park was inherited in 1886 by **1st Baron Redesdale**. During the 1860s he worked for the Foreign Office in Russia, Japan and China and fell in love with the oriental landscape, which directly influenced his design for the arboretum.

He died in 1916 and was **succeeded by David Mitford, 2nd Baron Redesdale**, who was **father of**

the six infamous Mitford sisters. They lived at Batsford during World War I and **Nancy Mitford** based the early part of her novel **Love in a Cold Climate** on their time at Batsford. **Another of the sisters, Diana**, married the **British fascist leader, Oswald Mosley**. The marriage took place in Germany at the **home of the Nazi propaganda minister, Joseph Goebbels** and the **guest of honour was Adolf Hitler**. In 1919 the estate was sold to cover death duties to **Gilbert Wills, 1st Baron Dulverton**, an **heir to the Wills tobacco fortune**.

After being neglected during and after World War II, the arboretum was revived by the **2nd Baron Dulverton**. In February 1992 he died leaving the Arboretum to the Batsford Foundation, a charitable trust set up to promote research and education into conservation, gardens and architecture, which runs the arboretum today. The rest of the Batsford Estate is still owned by the Wills family.

Batsford Arboretum, looking down
on the house at Batsford Park.

Credit: Cotswolds Tourism/ © Emma Bidmead

Paul's daughters Tydwen and Eirys
at Batsford Arboretum.

The Tallest Gravity-Fed Fountain in the World

Stanway House, a Jacobean manor house, **near the village of Stanway in Gloucestershire**, was **owned by Tewkesbury Abbey for 800 years** and for **the last 500 years by the Tracy family** and their descendants, the **Earls of Wemyss and March. J.M. Barrie, creator of Peter Pan**, was a frequent visitor during summers in the 1920s, until 1932.

Stanway House is also **home to the Stanway Fountain**, which was opened on 5 June 2004. **The single-jet fountain, which rises to over 300 feet, is the tallest fountain in Britain, the tallest gravity-fed fountain in the world and the second tallest fountain in Europe.** The fountain has a 2 inch bronze nozzle and is driven from a 100,000-gallon reservoir. The 12 inch diameter pipe which feeds the fountain is 2 kilometres long.

The current Earl, also known as **Lord Neidpath**, as a teenager was a **Page of Honour to Queen Elizabeth the Queen Mother**. He has also been a supporter of UKIP, donating over £50,000, and in 1992 led a 3000-strong march through Cheltenham to protest against Conservative President of the Board of Trade, **Michael Heseltine**'s plans to close coal mines.

The Best Training Facility in British Jump Racing

One of the **UK's most successful racehorse trainers, Jonjo O'Neill**, has his legendary training facility at **Jackdaws Castle, Temple Guiting**. O'Neill won the **Cheltenham Gold Cup** and the **Champion Hurdles as a Jockey** and the **Cheltenham Gold Cup** and **Grand National as a trainer**. Spread across 500 acres of the Cotswold countryside, Jackdaws Castle has three grass gallops, two all-weather gallops of five-furlongs and one-mile, schooling grounds featuring series of hurdles, brush hurdles and regular chasing fences, an equine swimming pool, an indoor school, an equine solarium, two yards and a covered barn full of stables to house the horses. It is **arguably the finest training facility in British jump racing**. The facility is owned by **Irish racehorse owner JP McManus**, who is a **former shareholder in Manchester United.**

The Highest Lock
on The Thames

The **highest lock on the Thames is St John's Lock**, at **Lechlade,** where there is a **statue of Old Father Thames** overlooking the boating activities. The **first lock on this site was built in 1790**. The lock and its adjoining bridge are named after a priory **dedicated to St John the Baptist**, which has long since disappeared.

The statue was made in 1854 for the **Crystal Palace at Hyde Park**. It was rescued from the fire at the Palace in 1936, and in 1958 the statue was **moved near the river's source, The Thames Head at Trewsbury Mead** near the **village of Coates**. Sady, the statue was vandalised there so it was moved to its current location in 1974.

Lechlade has hosted a music festival since 2011. In 2015, the headline act was Status Quo.

The Collapsed Viaduct Disaster

Stanway viaduct at Toddington is the **largest anywhere on a UK heritage railway** with 15 arches, 42 feet above the valley floor. It is now **part of the Gloucester and Warwickshire Steam Railway,** but was built by the GWR on a new line **linking Cheltenham with Stratford on Avon** to allow GWR direct communication between the South West and Midlands.

On Friday 13th November 1903, **disaster struck** when four men died and seven were injured after **three arches collapsed during construction.**

Just after 8am, without warning, no. 10 arch, which had been completed a few days earlier, collapsed soon after its timber supports had been removed. As it fell to the ground it brought down with it a 14-ton steam crane, which was lifting materials from ground level. The noise was heard over a mile away, according to local newspaper reports, and it brought workers rushing over immediately to help rescue anyone who might be trapped under the debris.

Miraculously, the driver of the steam crane - a man named Smith - survived and he was placed under arch no. 9 while the rescuers continued to retrieve a trapped worker. While this was going on, arch no. 9 collapsed equally suddenly, again **burying the unfortunate Mr. Smith**. While he was being dug out, arch no. 8 then collapsed. **Mr Smith was still alive when he emerged from the chaos but, perhaps unsurprisingly, he later died from his injuries** after he was taken to Winchcombe hospital. Three other men died in the disaster and seven were injured.

The Winchcombe Meteorite

The **Winchcombe meteorite** is a rare carbonaceous meteorite which **crashed onto a driveway in the Gloucestershire town** after its **spectacular fireball lit up the skies over the UK** in February 2021. It was found to contain **extra-terrestrial water and organic compounds** that reveal insights into the origin of Earth's oceans.

It was recovered after only 12 hours, meaning it is much less likely the water was contaminated by the earth's atmosphere. **Scientists believe the meteorite dates back to the very beginning of the Solar System, some 6.4 billion years ago,** and is pristine enough to rival asteroid samples taken directly from space. **After a fragment of the meteorite was put on display at the Winchcombe Museum, visitor numbers trebled.**

5.   ANIMALS

The Penguin Millionaire and the Birds with Disgusting Table Manners

Birdland Park & Gardens in **Bourton-on-the-Water**, Gloucestershire, first opened in 1957, and was started by **Len Hill**, a local **Cotswold builder** who was often **referred to as the Penguin Millionaire.**

There are **around 500 exotic birds, of over 130 different species**, contained within more than 150 open aviaries, in nine acres of parkland which provides a picturesque canopy for the winding River Windrush. **It contains the only breeding group for King Penguins in England, Wales or Ireland.**

The current site **housed a trout farm** when Birdland took over occupancy and this has been incorporated into the attraction. **Prior to this the site was a poplar tree plantation owned by Bryant and May for the production of matchsticks.**

As part of their **Birds Behaving Badly** Week in February 2019, Head keeper **Alistair Keen** revealed some interesting facts about their residents, saying: "Despite their often angelic reputations, birds are definitely among the worst behaved animals on the planet, with some truly disgusting table manners."

"The **marabou stork urinates on itself in order to cool its legs, fulmar chicks aim projectile vomit at the face of any potential threats** and **oxpecker birds will open old wounds on cattle in Africa in order to drink their blood.**"

"Swallows and housemartins use their own spit to build nests and the lilac-breasted roller vomits on its own chicks to deter would-be predators," he added.

Videos of Birdland's King Penguin, Spike, went viral during the Covid lockdown, being viewed over 25,000 times. He now has over 15,000 followers on his own Facebook page.

The UK's Only Crocodile Zoo

'**Crocodiles of the World**' in **Brize Norton**, Oxfordshire is **the UK's first and only crocodile zoo**. It is home to a wide range of crocodiles, including Siamese crocodiles from Cambodia, Chinese alligators, Nile crocodiles and American alligators. **It is home to over 100 crocodiles from 14 crocodilian species, making it the largest collection of crocodiles in the UK.**

Founded by crocodile specialist and former carpenter **Shaun Foggett** in 2011, 'Crocodiles of the World' is the result of a lifetime dedicated to the care and breeding of crocodiles. From a childhood collecting exotic pets and reptiles, Shaun has travelled the world learning about these incredible animals, and is now recognised as one of the few licensed and trusted crocodile keepers in the country. The zoo is also home to a number of other reptiles including a 2 metre crocodile monitor lizard, alligator snapping turtle, Meller's chameleons, pig-nosed turtle, and other reptile species. 'Crocodiles of the World' has **been the subject of a number of television programmes** in the past, including a **Channel 5** three-part documentary, '**Croc Man**', about Shaun's journey, which first aired in 2011.

Television Presenter's Home to Rare Breeds

Television presenter Adam Henson runs **Cotswold Farm Park at Guiting Power.** He follows in the footsteps of his father Joe, who opened the Farm Park to the public in 1971 after starting to **keep rare breeds**, including **Gloucestershire Old Spot** pigs. Joe founded the **Rare Breeds Survival Trust in 1973**, since when **no UK-native breed has become extinct. Joe received an MBE** in the 2011 **Queen's Birthday Honours for services to conservation.**

The Trout Farm Producing 10 Million Trout a Year

Bibury Trout Farm, in the heart of the beautiful **Cotswold village of Bibury**, is **one of the oldest**, and certainly the most attractive, trout farms in the country. **Founded in 1902** by the naturalist **Arthur Severn**, it covers 15 acres. Primarily a working farm, breeding and rearing high quality Rainbow and Brown Trout for restocking angling waters, it has welcomed visitors since 1965, who can see the water come alive as the fish are fed and learn about the life of a trout! Each year **up to 10 million Rainbow Trout are spawned**, up to one third being sold to outlets throughout Britain and occasionally abroad. The remainder are grown on and sold principally to restock rivers, lakes and reservoirs throughout the country. Numerous ducks, swans, Kingfishers, geese and other wildlife including the rare water vole can be seen and fed in the beautiful surroundings.

A family enjoying their time at Bibury Trout Farm.

Credit: Cotswolds Tourism/ © Nick Turner Photography

The Cotswold Chickens with Coloured Eggs

The origins of the Old Cotswold Legbar chicken go back nearly 100 years, when botanist and explorer, **Clarence Elliott** returned from an expedition to **Patagonia in 1927** with three blue egg laying **Chilean chickens, or Araucanas.**

The fourth bird was a cock, who **met with an unfortunate end during the voyage, at the hands of the ship's cook**, who spoke little English. The cook misunderstood Elliott's instructions to, **'give the cock some supper'** because it was making a terrible noise during a violent storm. The hapless bird became supper himself!

Elliott **gave the three hens to a friend at Cambridge, Professor Reginald Punnett**, who was director of the University's breeding programme. The professor was **assisted by Michael Pease.** A separate poultry unit was set up in 1930, headed by Pease, and one of the by-products of Punnett's experiments in producing auto-sexing poultry was the Cream or Crested Legbar, which carried the genes from Elliott's three hens and **laid blue/green eggs**. Punnett introduced these Crested Cream Legbars at the London Dairy Show in 1947.

An undergraduate at Cambridge at the time of Punnett's poultry experiments called **John Croome** carried on breeding the Cream Legbars following the dispersal of the Cambridge breeding facility in the early 1950's until his death in 1988. **Fortunately, the Cream Legbars were saved from extinction** because Croome had given some hatching eggs to David Applegarth in Yorkshire.

In 1989, **Philip Lee-Woolf** and **wife Janet**, formed the **Clarence Court egg business, at Millhampost Farm, Winchcombe**. The business name was coined from the **Queen Mother's home, Clarence House**, because rumour had it that the **Queen Mother enjoyed a blue egg for breakfast**. Their stunning new eggs were to bring a touch of elegance and refinement to what had become a boring utility product.

Philip was asked by **Fortnum & Mason** to supply the **famous London grocer** with eau de nil (light green) coloured eggs, which would be a perfect match for the store's elegant décor.

He obtained some hatching eggs from **David Applegarth** and bred a flock of several hundred Cream Legbars. A few years later, following a move to Broadway, he introduced other bloodlines to Punnett's Cream Legbar and the Old Cotswold

Legbar was born. She soon took centre stage, producing elegant pastel shades of blue, eau-de-nil, celadon (jade green) and pink.

Cotswold Legbar eggs are the preferred choice for many of London's upmarket stores and top chefs, including **Jamie Oliver**, **Rick Stein** and **Tom Parker-Bowles**. Cotswold Legbar Chickens continue to be bred by Legbars of Broadway.

The War Pigeon

Kenley Lass was a war pigeon who **received the Dickin Medal** in 1945 from the People's Dispensary for Sick Animals **for bravery in service during the Second World War**. The Dickin Medal was instituted in 1943 in the United Kingdom by **Maria Dickin** to **honour the work of animals in World War II**. Kenley Lass received the award after she was the **first pigeon selected to accompany an agent into enemy-occupied France** in October 1940 to see if such a bird could reach home in Britain with secret messages. **The MI6 agent, codename Philippe**, was dropped by parachute with instructions to cover a distance of 9 miles on foot, avoid detection and gather intelligence before using Kenley Lass to **send it back to Britain.**

Eleven days later, Philippe released Kenley Lass and she arrived in Shropshire at 3pm the same day after travelling over 300 miles. Following her success more pigeons were trained and selected for this type of wartime work. On 16th February 1941, Kenley Lass was used again for a secret mission in France.

She was bred in Poynton, Cheshire and later sold to Donald Cole from Cirencester.

6.   PEOPLE

I'm A Chipping Campden Celebrity

Former Culture Secretary, novelist and **'I'm A Celebrity' contestant Nadine Dorries** lived in the 14th century **Woolstaplers Hall** in **Chipping Campden** before becoming an MP. For **hundreds of years it was a Wool Exchange**, attracting merchants from London and **as far afield as Florence**, to buy **Cotswold fleeces** for shipment around the world. It was later a museum. Television presenter and pasta sauce promoter **Loyd Grossman**, who knows more than a bit about culture as a former Chair of Culture Northwest and English Heritage Commissioner, moved to the town in 2021.

Prue's Pub Crawls

'Great British Bake Off' star **Prue Leith** has **lived in the Cotswolds, near Moreton-in-Marsh,** for **over 40 years.** She sold her long-term home in 2021 for **£10 million**, downsizing to a barn conversion nearby.

She caused a stir when she revealed that she liked nothing better than a **pub crawl in the Cotswolds with her husband John Playfair**. The chef says she rides pillion on his **Harley Davidson** to visit the many watering holes near her home, with a particular **favourite being the Queen's Head at Stow-on-the-Wold.**

The Chipping Norton Set

The **Chipping Norton set** is a **group of media**, **political** and **show-business** acquaintances who have homes near the Cotswold market town of **Chipping Norton in Oxfordshire**. The group gained notoriety in the wake of the News International phone hacking scandal, which directly involved some members of the group.

The term **"Chipping Norton set"** was **included in the 19th edition of Brewer's Dictionary of Phrase and Fable**, published in 2012. Members of the set include **racehorse trainer Charlie Brooks** and **his wife Rebecca, the former Chief Executive of News International; former Prime Minister David Cameron** and **his wife Samantha; former Top Gear presenter Jeremy Clarkson; Rupert Murdoch's daughter Elisabeth** and her **PR tycoon former husband Matthew Freud; Charles Dunstone, co-founder of Carphone Warehouse** and **Alex James, formerly of pop group Blur.**

The town of Chipping Norton, which has become a centre for a group of famous and powerful friends.

Credit: Cotswolds Tourism / © Anthony Paul Photography

Poet Pam is a Cotswolds Character

Poet Pam Ayres has lived near Cirencester for many years. Her poem **"Oh, I Wish I'd Looked After Me Teeth"**, was **voted into the Top 10 of a BBC poll** to find the nation's **100 Favourite Comic Poems** in 1998. She presented a **Channel 5** series called **'The Cotswolds with Pam Ayres'** in 2021, which was recommissioned as **'The Cotswolds and Beyond'** in 2022.

Coates Tales

The **village of Coates**, near Cirencester, is **home to DIY SOS presenter Nick Knowles** and **former Arsenal & England footballer Tony Adams**, who appeared on **'Strictly Come Dancing'** in 2022. Knowles moved to the area from Chiswick in West London in 2017. In 2022 he caused controversy when he went on a **Twitter rampage over a broken McDonald's Milkshake machine** in Cirencester. Adams has lived in the village since 2004 after buying a £2 million home there.

The Dewhurst Tycoon and Master of the Horse

Stowell Park, a **6000-acre estate near Northleach**, has been **home to the Vestey family** since 1923. The Vesteys are **one of Britain's richest families** with a **fortune estimated to be around £700 million**. Much of their wealth comes from food production and **at one point they owned the Dewhursts chain of butchers shops**. **Lord Sam Vestey**, who died in 2021, was **Chairman of Cheltenham Racecourse** for many years and was **Master of The Horse** (a largely ceremonial role) to **HM Queen Elizabeth II** from 1999-2018. **MP for The Cotswolds, Sir Geoffrey Clifton-Brown**, is related to the Vesteys on his late mother's side.

The Cirencester Teacher Who Challenged Maggie

An exchange on 24th May 1983 between **Diana Gould, an English schoolteacher** from Cirencester and **former Women's Royal Naval Service meteorological officer**, and **Prime Minister Margaret Thatcher** was voted in 1999 as **one of Britain's most memorable television moments**. Appearing as a member of the public on **BBC** Nationwide's **'On the Spot'** live election special, **Gould confronted the Prime Minister** over the **sinking of the Belgrano**, an **Argentine warship, during the 1982 Falklands War.**

Mrs Gould believed the sinking had wrecked a chance for peace. She became interested in that part of the world when studying Geography at Cambridge.

The exchange between Thatcher and Gould became iconic, remembered because of Gould's persistence in asking why Thatcher had given the order, which seemed to rattle the Prime Minister. It was described as **"the day Margaret Thatcher met her match"**. Mrs Gould died in 2011, aged 85.

The Ambassador who ran a Town Council

Peter Jay, formerly the **UK's Ambassador to the United States** from 1977-79 and **son-in-law of former Prime Minister Jim Callaghan**, was a **town councillor in the Oxfordshire town of Woodstock and Mayor** in 2008. During his career he was also the **founding chairman of breakfast television broadcaster Tv-am** and **chief of staff to disgraced publishing tycoon Robert Maxwell**.

The Beckhams and Their Underground Tunnel

Former England football captain David Beckham and his wife, former Spice Girl Victoria, own a converted farmhouse in the **Oxfordshire village of Great Tew**, near **Chipping Norton**, which they bought in 2016 for £6.15 million. The house has a large swimming pool, tennis court, treehouse and even a football pitch and overlooks the wide-open countryside. In 2020, the couple were granted planning consent to **build an underground tunnel to link their wine cellar at the main house with a large garage** near the entrance to their home.

The Tetrapak Billionaires

Hans Rausing, grandson of the **founder of the Tetrapak packaging empire**, and **his wife Julia** live at **Lasborough Park near Tetbury**. Over the years they have **given hundreds of millions of pounds to charities through their family trust**, including over **£500,000 in 2022 to preserve the cloisters at Gloucester Cathedral**.

The Archers

Cirencester has produced two **gold medal-winning archers**. **Phoebe Paterson Pine won Gold** at the **2020 Paralympics in Japan** in the women's Individual Compound.

Fellow Archer Ella Gibson won a Gold medal in two consecutive World Cup stages in the 2022 Hyundai Archery World Cup for female compound archery – something which has never been achieved before.

The Dynasty Star

Former Dynasty actress Emma Samms, who played **Fallon Carrington Colby**, lives near **Nailsworth in Gloucestershire** with her husband, **GB News anchor and former BBC presenter Simon McCoy.** She suffered with symptoms of Long Covid after contracting the virus in March 2020 and has campaigned for the condition to be taken more seriously.

She **first appeared** in American daytime soap opera **'General Hospital'** in 1982, playing the **character of Holly Sutton.** She made occasional appearances on the programme over the years. In September 2020, she reprised her role as Holly Sutton for one episode in a scene that revealed her character, who was presumed dead, was actually being held prisoner somewhere in Monte Carlo. Samms had to shoot the scene from her own home due to the coronavirus pandemic. Her return was delayed by her bout of Long Covid and she finally rejoined the soap in October 2022.

The Cotswolds'
'Smooth Operator'

Nigerian-born **pop star Sade**, who had her greatest success in the 1980s with singles **'Smooth Operator'** and **'Your Love Is King'** and the album **'Diamond Life'**, has lived near Stroud since 2005 after buying a run-down cottage to renovate. Despite being described in the media as living as a 'virtual recluse', **locals have reported bumping into her in Waitrose** and her joining in singing Happy Birthday to them in the local pub! She has **sold 50 million records worldwide** and in 2012 the Daily Mail reported that she had **even outsold Adele in the US over the previous 12 months.**

Lily's Lair

Pop singer Lily Allen bought the 17th century **Old Overtown House** in the **hamlet of Overtown**, near **Cranham**, with **then husband Sam Cooper** for £3 million in 2010. Her **actor father Keith** lives in nearby **Slad**. She put the house up for sale in June 2016 for £4.2 million. In 2016, The Daily Mail reported that Allen and Cooper hadn't been seen together in public for over a year and had stopped wearing wedding rings. They divorced in 2018 in another example of **'The Curse of The Cotswolds'**, where celebrity relationships seem to break down after moving to the area. Others who have suffered the same fate include **Liz Hurley, Kate Moss, Jeremy Clarkson** and **Kate Winslet**.

Lily Allen isn't the only musical connection there is with Cranham. The composer, **Gustav Holst**, who was born in Cheltenham, came up with a tune which he named **'Cranham'** to which he set the words of the poem **'In The Bleak Midwinter'**. It became the popular Christmas Carol. At the time Holst was living in Cranham and the property he lived in was **subsequently named 'Midwinter Cottage'** to commemorate this.

Film Star's Titanic Renovation Project

Actress **Kate Winslet** who **starred in Titanic**, the **second highest-grossing film of all time**, lived at **Church Westcote, near Burford**. Winslet bought The Manor at Church Westcote with her then husband, film director **Sam Mendes** in 2002 for £3.3 million, **outbidding fellow actress Liz Hurley** and paying £0.5 million over the asking price. It had been empty for some time following the death of its **previous owner Raoul Millais**, a wildlife artist. Council planning officers recommended refusal of the couple's plans to renovate the property in June 2003, but councillors voted for a site visit and gave their approval the following month. Winslet and Mendes split in 2010 and these days she lives at **West Wittering** in **West Sussex** with third husband **Edward Abel-Smith** - a **nephew of Sir Richard Branson** who previously changed his name to **Ned Rocknroll**.

Supermodel's Cotswold Property Witnessed in Film Star's Court Case

Supermodel Kate Moss lives at **Little Faringdon, near Lechlade**. She left London and moved to the Cotswolds permanently in 2021, having bought the 10 bedroom property over a decade earlier for £2 million.

The property provided the backdrop when Moss gave evidence by video link in the Johnny Depp v Amber Heard court case. Moss, who dated Depp between 1994 and 1998, denied claims by Ms Heard that Depp had once pushed her down a flight of stairs.

Her wedding to **rockstar Jamie Hince** at **St Peter's Church, Southrop** in 2011 caused some local controversy when roads were shut off to residents. Villagers and guests had to use permits to enter Little Faringdon, Oxfordshire, and Southrop, Gloucestershire. The couple were said to have held a festival-themed, three-day party. The pair divorced in 2016.

The Colourful Character with a Shade of Grey

Laurence Llewellyn-Bowen, the interior designer and star of the **BBC and Channel Four programme 'Changing Rooms',** lives in a 16th century, Grade II listed manor house at **Siddington,** just **outside Cirencester** and has a showroom in the former police station in Cirencester town centre.

Llewelyn-Bowen's home was **once owned by John Roberts,** a founding member of the Quaker movement who fought with **Oliver Cromwell** during the Civil War and **was later imprisoned in Gloucester Castle.** The sprawling grounds include a 17th Century Quaker burial ground.

In 2021, Llewelyn-Bowen was ordered by Cotswold District Council to paint a new annex at his home in 'ultra-neutral' Dulux Flake Grey to meet planning regulations, perhaps concerned he would be using his trademark bold colours.

Over the past few years, Laurence **has worked on the Blackpool Illuminations, designing a number of spectacular features and installations,** and in September 2022 was invited to **do the honours at the official switch-on ceremony.**

The Bowls Champion... and Parish Council Chairman

Twice World Outdoor Singles champion and **three times World Indoor Singles bowls champion Tony Allcock** lives at **Guiting Power** and is **Chairman of its Parish Council.** In total, he **won 17 gold medals on the world stage.**

Before becoming a **full-time bowls player, Allcock was Head Teacher at St Rose's special school in Stroud** and prior to that he held the same position at another special school in Tewkesbury. After retiring from playing, he became **Chief Executive of Bowls England.** He was **awarded an MBE for services to sport** and **later an OBE for administration in sport and service to charity.** He is a keen dog breeder and is the **current chairman of the Kennel Club.**

Allcock says his **proudest achievement is coaching 70 year-old Ruth Small to the gold medal in the visually-impaired women's singles bowls at the 2002 Commonwealth Games.**

The Three Duchesses
of Beaufort

The **Duke of Beaufort** lives at **Badminton House**, near **Chipping Sodbury** in South Gloucestershire, on the **52,000-acre Badminton estate**. It is thought that **army officers in 1863 played a version of the game of badminton** at the house and perhaps **this is how the sport became commonly referred to as badminton**. The House's Entrance Hall reflects the dimensions of a modern **badminton court**.

In 2017, it was reported that, confusingly, due to aristocratic protocols there would be three Duchesses of Beaufort. The 12th Duke was about to remarry, so both his ex-wife and his new wife would have the title of Duchess, as would his stepmother!

Badminton House has been the family's seat since the late 17th century. It was previously **Raglan Castle in Monmouthshire**.

The Cirencester Astronomer

Astronomer and Quaker, Elizabeth Brown was born in 1830 and lived in Cirencester. She **specialised in solar observation, especially sunspots and solar eclipses.**

Her father, **Thomas Brown**, an amateur astronomer, introduced her to science, including observing sunspots and taking meteorological measurements, notably of rainfall. She took over her father's meteorological observations from 1871 until his death aged 91 in 1883. After his death, she began to travel the world to make observations of solar eclipses, visiting Russia, Norway, Spain and the Caribbean. She published two anonymous accounts of her travels, **'In Pursuit of a Shadow'** and **'Caught in the Tropics'**, published in 1887 and 1890 respectively. Her daily recording of sunspots, including meticulous drawings, earned her a distinguished reputation.

In 1890, she helped to **found the British Astronomical Association** to coordinate the research of amateur astronomers. On its foundation, she immediately **became the Director of its Solar Section** and a member of its governing council. She strongly encouraged other women to become astronomers, especially solar astronomers. In 1892 she and two other women were proposed for **fellowship of the Royal Astronomical Society.** However, none of the women received enough votes from the male members of the Society and were not elected. She was, however, one of the first women Fellows of the Royal Meteorological Society.

7. FOOD & DRINK

Henry Who?

It has been **claimed that the drink Orange Juice and Lemonade being called a 'Henry'** originated in the **Corinium Hotel in Cirencester**. The story is that a regular called Henry always asked for the drink after a night on the booze. The name is only widely-used in Gloucestershire and people asking for it outside the county are often met with blank looks!

Another suggested explanation is that it relates to the drink Orange and Bitter Lemon being called a **'St Clements'** after the **nursery rhyme, 'Oranges and Lemons'.** Some suggest it is named after **Henry VIII**, who **Pope Clement VII excommunicated from the Catholic Church** following his **marriage to Ann Boleyn.**

We prefer the **Gloucestershire version!**

Chicken in the Basket

The **Mill Inn at Withington**, 10 kilometres south east of Cheltenham, is credited with introducing the **'chicken and chips in a basket'** meal in the 1960s. It is still served at the pub today. **Celebrity chef Tom Kerridge**, who was brought up in Gloucester, recalls driving out to enjoy the dish at The Mill when he had just passed his driving test and has come up with his own recipe for a spicier version!

One of the Best Wines in the World

In January 2023, Cotswold-based family-owned boutique winemakers, **Woodchester Valley Vineyard**, won the **'Master' medal at the Global Sauvignon Blanc Masters awards** in the £20-£30 category of unoaked entries.

The wine, a 2021 vintage, **beat entrants from** more traditional winemaking countries such as **France, Italy and New Zealand.** At the time it retailed for £21.95 on the vineyard's website. The wine was made using vines only planted in 2015 on a virgin site at the company's 58 acre vineyard near Stroud.

The judges said the result is a "perfect example of why we taste blind - partly to leave any preconceptions behind us, and partly for the absolute joy of surprise when something unexpected turns out to be wonderful."

They added: "And this wine was, indeed, wonderful. It starts with an intense gooseberry nose, building to reveal undertones of ripe lemon. On the palate there is bright, taut acidity and a juicy mouthfeel."

8.   EVENTS, SPORT & ENTERTAINMENT

Shin Kicking

Shin-kicking is a combat sport that involves two contestants attempting to **kick each other on the shin to force their opponent to the ground**. It is arguably the **biggest attraction at Robert Dover's Cotswold Olimpicks**. The event is held annually in the early summer at **Dover's Hill**, just outside Chipping Campden, and draws thousands of spectators. Shin-kicking originated in England in the early 17th Century and has been described as **an English martial art**. It was included in the 1951 revival of the **Cotswold Olimpicks**, which now features the **World Shin-Kicking Championships.**

The matches are observed by a referee, or stickler, who determines the match score in a best of three competition. **The phrase 'a stickler for the rules' is believed to have originated from this practice**. Steel toe caps are now banned, and the use of straw is allowed to pad shins.

The Cotswold Olimpicks, held on the Friday after Spring Bank Holiday, **celebrated its 400th anniversary** in 2012 - a few months before the London Olympics - and the event drew **international media attention.**

Shin kicking taking place at the
Cotswold Olimpicks.

Credit: Cotswolds Tourism/ © Nick Turner Photography

Woolsack Racing

The **Tetbury Woolsack Races** are an annual sporting event in the **Cotswold town of Tetbury**, held each year on the **Whitsun Bank Holiday Monday**.

It is thought that the races **originated in the 17th Century** by young drovers showing off to local women by **running up the hill carrying a woolsack**. An official race day has been going for over 30 years now with **world records entered in the 'Guinness Book of Records'**.

Competitors race up and down the steepest street in the town carrying a full woolsack on their back. The races take place on **Gumstool Hill** between two public houses, the **Royal Oak (the bottom of the hill)** and **the Crown (at the top)**. People can take part either as individuals or as part of a team. The individuals race up the hill, the teams (with four members swapping places at each end of the course) race up and down the hill twice.

The **men race with a 60-pound woolsack** and **women have 35-pound sacks**. There are also **youth races, where boys ages 16–18 races with a 30-pound sack**, and a children's class. The weight of the children's woolsack is unspecified but is probably about the same as a pillow.

Regular competitors include local rugby teams, the British Army and the Norfolk Mountain Rescue Team.

Competitors in the Tetbury Woolsack Races.

Credit: Cotswolds Tourism/ © Nick Turner Photography

Football in the River at Bourton

This **world-famous event** happens in the **River Windrush** at **Bourton-on-the-Water** every **August Bank Holiday.** Thousands of people line up alongside the riverbank to **watch two teams from Bourton Rovers Football Club battle it out for the honours.**

Goalposts are set up in the river with the **pitch approximately 50 metres long by 9 metres wide.** The game is **15 minutes each way with no rules** apart from that players will splash the crowd. **The river itself is a shallow 10 inches deep at most with a pebbled bed.** As the river is fresh running, it is as cold at that time as it is in the winter.

The tradition is **said to have started about 120 years ago** when drinkers in the riverside Kingsbridge pub got bored one day and decided to **stage an impromptu match in the water.**

The event has **attracted many celebrities** over the years, including **Griff Rhys Jones** taking part as part of his **Cotswold TV show**, as well as **Adam Henson** and **Paddy McGuinness.**

The annual football match in the River
Windrush at Bourton-on-the-Water.

Credit: Cotswolds Tourism/ © Anthony Paul Photography

Father Brown's Villages

Father Brown is a popular drama **based on the stories by GK Chesterton** about a **crime-solving Roman Catholic priest** in the 1950s. The television show first aired on **BBC1** in 2013, with **Mark Williams** as the eponymous priest with a knack for solving mysteries. Williams is perhaps **best known for playing Arthur Weasley** in seven of the **Harry Potter films.** The easy-watching crime drama is enduringly popular daytime viewing with nine series aired as of the end of 2022.

Filming ten episodes for the first series of the programme began in summer 2012. The drama is based in the picture postcard **fictional Cotswold village of 'Kembleford'**

The **church of Saints Peter and Paul in the village of Blockley** served as St Mary's Roman Catholic Church in the series, with the village vicarage turned into a 1950s presbytery for the priest's residence. The church yard was covered in artificial snow for the show's Christmas special at the end of 2017.

The village of **Guiting Power** was also used as a filming location for the fictional village and the

former Moreton-in-Marsh hospital has been used for the interiors of Father Brown's kitchen, study and presbytery, as well as Kembleford's police station.

The village of Blockley, where
Father Brown was filmed.

Credit: Cotswolds Tourism/ © Anthony Paul Photography

The Pop Concert in the 'Cathedral of the Cotswolds'

Singer/songwriter Steve Winwood, who has had hits as part of the **Spencer Davis Group** and **Traffic** as well as solo success, lives in the **Cotswold village of Turkdean** near **Bourton-on-the-Water**. On a number of occasions, he has performed at a **charity concert in nearby Northleach Church** with other **big names including Led Zeppelin's Robert Plant. Winwood's daughter Mary-Clare is married to Ben Elliott, former Co-Chair of the Conservative Party and nephew of Camilla, Queen Consort.**

Northleach Church is known as the **'Cathedral of the Cotswolds'. It has stood at the heart of the town for at least 800 years.** One of the Cotswold historic 'wool' churches, it is celebrated for its light and the almost complete absence of stained glass windows.

Northleach Church, known as the
'Cathedral of the Cotswolds'.

Credit: Cotswolds Tourism/ © Nick Turner Photography

Nailsworth's Gold
Post Boxes

There are a **pair of gold-painted EIIR post boxes** at the entrance to a Tesco store in **Nailsworth**. They **mark the achievement of Pete Reed**, an **Olympic rower who won gold** as part of the Men's Coxless Four team on 4th August 2012 at the London Olympics. **Reed is a three-times Olympic gold medallist** – earning gold in the Men's coxless four at the 2008 and 2012 Olympics, and then a gold medal in the Men's eight at the 2016 Olympics in Rio de Janeiro. **He has won five gold medals and three silver medals** at the World Championships. Although born in Seattle, USA, he was raised in Nailsworth.

Co-author Paul James with Nailsworth's two gold post boxes in 2012.

The Jillywood Experience

Novelist Jilly Cooper has lived in the **village of Bisley near Stroud** since 1982. Her **'Rutshire Chronicles'** series of racy novels, including **'Riders'**, **'Rivals'** and **'Mount'**, is based in the **fictional county of Rutshire**, which is **based on the Cotswolds**. She has acknowledged that the **central character of Rupert Campbell-Black is based in part upon Andrew Parker Bowles, the former husband of Camilla, The Queen Consort.**

In 2006, a minibus tour of Cotswolds celebrities' homes was created and named the **'Jillywood Experience'** after Jilly, who was its most popular subject.

The First Vegan Football Club

Forest Green Rovers FC, **based at Nailsworth**, is the **world's first UN-certified carbon-neutral soccer club. Owned by New Age Traveller turned renewable energy tycoon Dale Vince,** the Club serves Vegan food to players and fans.

FGR is powered by 100% green energy from Vince's company Ecotricity, some of which is generated by the solar panels on the stadium roof. The team plays on an organic pitch, which is cut by a solar-powered robot lawnmower, and all rainwater that falls on the stands or on the pitch is recycled to minimise the club's use of mains water. FGR has electric car charging facilities at the stadium, to encourage fans to travel to games sustainably. In 2021, the team became the first in the world to play in a football kit made from a composite material consisting of recycled plastic and coffee grounds.

In 2018, The Sun branded the Club 'hypocrites' when it was revealed that players had tucked into a huge order of chicken, fish and chips after a match at Macclesfield, but a spokesman said Vegan rules only applied when at the Club and players were free to eat what they want to in their own time.

Cider with Rosie

The **poet, novelist and screenwriter Laurie Lee** was brought up in the **small village of Slad, near Stroud**, in Gloucestershire. His most famous work is his autobiographical novel **'Cider with Rosie'**, which recounts his childhood in the Slad Valley and depicts the hardships, pleasures and simplicity of rural life in the time of Lee's youth. He is buried in the village churchyard. The inscription on his gravestone reads **"He lies in the valley he loved"**.

Another literary connection is that the **poet T.S. Eliot's poem 'The Country Walk'** was **inspired by his fear of cows while on rambles in The Cotswolds!**

A picture of a young Laurie Lee, in
The Woolpack pub in Slad.

Credit: Cotswolds Tourism/ © Nick Turner Photography

The Cotswolds 'Mockumentary'

This Country is a **British 'mockumentary' sitcom**, first broadcast on **BBC Three** in February 2017. Created by, written by and starring siblings **Daisy May Cooper** and **Charlie Cooper**, the series is about the day-to-day lives of young people in rural Britain, focusing on two cousins living in an unnamed small village in the Cotswolds.

The Coopers play the central characters, **cousins Kerry** and **Lee 'Kurtan' Mucklowe**. Their father, **Paul Cooper**, plays **Kerry's father Martin Mucklowe**, while their uncle, **Trevor Cooper**, plays local man and antagonist **Len Clifton**.

The majority of scenes are **filmed in Northleach**, with others in **Stow-on-the-Wold** and **Fairford**. **The Coopers are from Cirencester. When they staged a preview of series three in their hometown, 25,000 people applied for the 400 tickets**. The town's population is approximately 20,000

The series has **won a host of awards**, including **'Best Scripted Comedy'** at the **British Academy Television Awards** in 2018. There have been three series of the programme.

The town square at Northleach, where
This Country was filmed.

Credit: Cotswolds Tourism/ © Anthony Paul Photography

The Rock Drummer Called Colin

Rock drummer **Cozy Powell** was **born in Cirencester** as **Colin Flooks** and was adopted. He started playing drums aged 12 in the school orchestra. The **first band Powell was in, called The Corals,** played at the youth clubs in Cirencester and nearby Latton. **During this time the band broke the world record for non-stop playing.** The stage name Cozy was taken from the US jazz drummer Cozy Cole.

Powell **made his name with major rock bands and artists** such as **The Jeff Beck Group, Rainbow, Michael Schenker Group, Gary Moore, Robert Plant, Brian May, Whitesnake, Emerson, Lake & Powell,** and **Black Sabbath.**

Powell appeared on at least 66 albums, with contributions on many other recordings, and **many rock drummers have cited him as a major influence.**

Powell died, aged 50, on 5th April 1998 following a car crash. A **memorial plaque at The Corn Hall in Cirencester** was unveiled on 7 January 2016, in a **ceremony led by Brian May, with Black Sabbath lead guitarist Tony Iommi, Whitesnake bassist**

Neil Murray and guitarist Bernie Marsden and singer Suzi Quatro in attendance.

The town council in Cirencester council took action after a **petition for a plaque to mark Powell's legacy,** which Italian music fan Rossella Amadori started in 2014, **attracted 3500 signatures.**

Record producer Mickie Most said, **"Musically, he was one of the best drummers we've ever had in this country."**

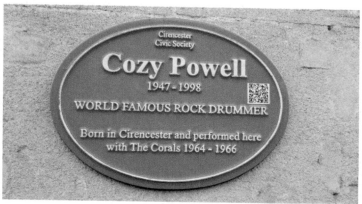

A plaque commemorating Cozy Powell,
at the Corn Hall in Cirencester.

Printed in Great Britain
by Amazon